Ava Rice
Gets Something Nice!

by JSB Morse

Copyright © 2023 by JSB Morse. All Rights Reserved. Printed in the United States of America.
Holy Scripture from Luke 6:38

This book was produced by Libertas Kids, an imprint of Code Publishing, Austin, TX. LibertasKids.com
ISBN 978-1-60020-097-7

In a land not far away, there lived a girl named Ava Rice,
Who had a love for money, her heart's only vice.

She'd steal from her brothers,
hoarding coins galore,
She dreamed of being the richest
and always wanting more.

One sunny day, Ava's grandpa came to town,
With a gift for the girl, both strange and profound.

The box had the shape of a 20-pound bean,
And it had odd writing on it, like nothing she'd seen.

Grandpa said "This box holds immeasurable worth,
In fact, it holds the greatest treasure on Earth!"
And the treasure was hers if she could open the box,
But she had to be clever to unlock the locks.

Ava tried everything, from saws to a hammer,
But the box wouldn't budge despite all the clamor.

It stayed tightly shut and Ava became irate,
So, she kicked it and smashed it with her mom's finest plate.

Then Ava had an idea: to decipher the text!
She researched old languages, feeling quite perplexed.
But learned it was Aramaic, a language of old,
And discovered the message that the box writing told.

The message on the box was clear and true,
"Give, and it shall be given to you."
A biblical lesson, so simple and sound,
It was like a golden rule that Ava had found.

She contemplated the message with a thoughtful stare,
Aware of her greed, a weight she couldn't bear.
With remorse in her heart, she would right her wrongs,
Return what she had taken and mend all the bonds.

At first it was hard to part with her cash.
When she spent it on others her teeth would all gnash.
But as time went on, she liked this new way of living,
She discovered the real joy in cheerfully giving.

She gave a nice toy to each of her brothers,
And she replaced that fine plate she'd destroyed of her mother's.

Then she branched out with her gift-giving grace,
To a friend, a kind word and a smile on her face.
Then she gave a hand, to an old lady in need,
Spreading love and compassion and goodwill indeed.

Then magically the box opened up with a click,
So Ava rushed over to look inside quick.
She had given to others so she would receive,
At least that's what the box led her to believe.

Ava looked inside the box with hope in her eyes,
But it was totally empty, to her sad surprise.

Inside the box was nothing at all,
She wanted to cry and she wanted to bawl.

Confronting her grandpa, she exclaimed, "You lied to me! This just isn't right; it's not how it should be!"

Her grandpa just smiled and nodded his head,
And took her in his arms and he lovingly said,
"My dear, my dear, all that glitters isn't gold,
Your kindness is worth more than anything that's sold."

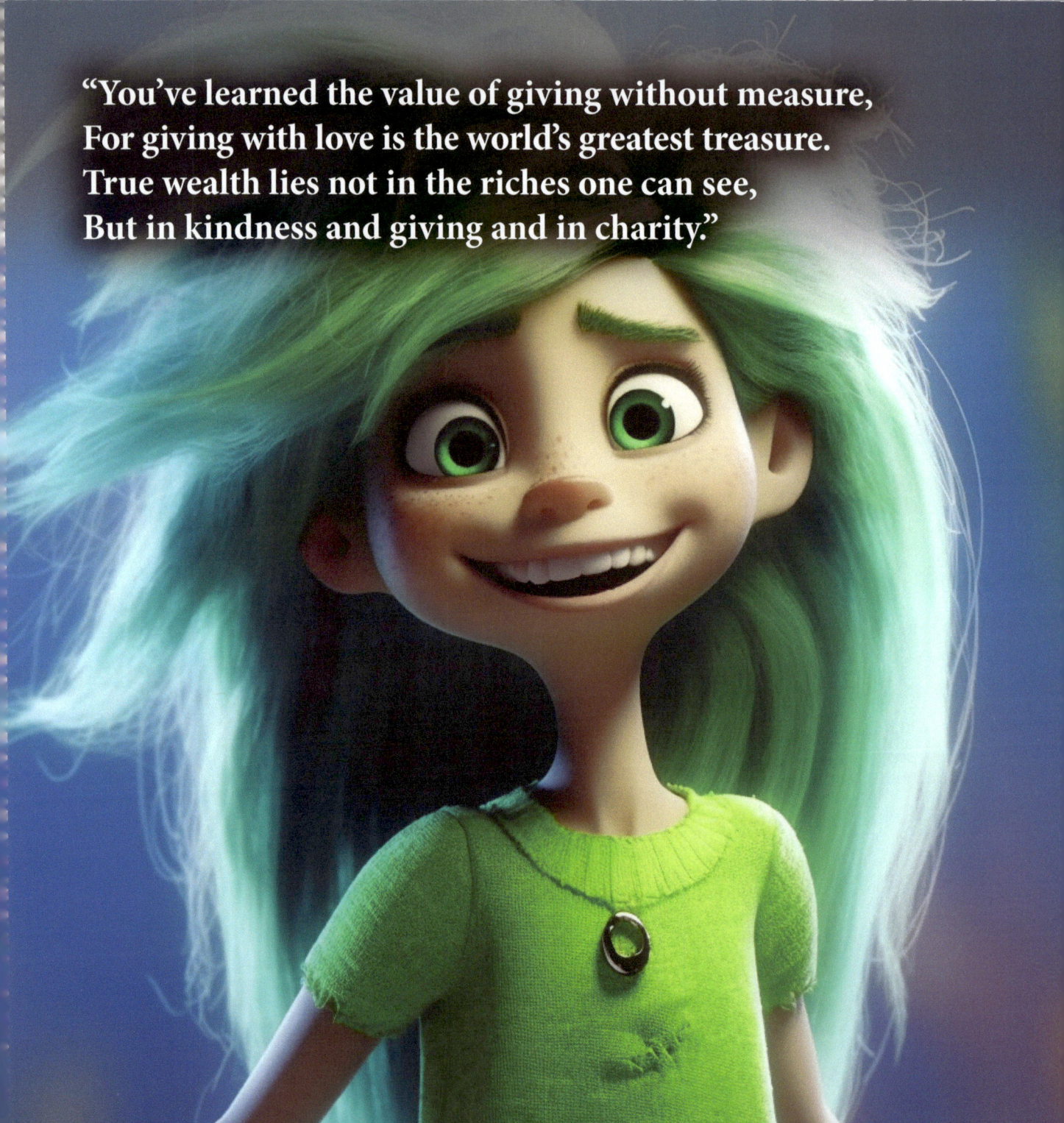

"You've learned the value of giving without measure,
For giving with love is the world's greatest treasure.
True wealth lies not in the riches one can see,
But in kindness and giving and in charity."

With a smile and a hug and a wink of his eye,
He turned to leave and gave a, "Goodbye!"
Ava said, "thank you" for the lesson she now knew,
But as he left with a smile, he said, "No, no, thank *you*."

THE END.

For more great stories, visit LibertasKids.com!

www.ingramcontent.com/pod-product-compliance
Lightning Source LLC
Chambersburg PA
CBHW041602070526
44586CB00003BA/60